I0003229

Paul Watson is a technology enthusiast and has massive experience in various technologies like Linux system administration, web application development, automation testing, build automation, continuous integration and deployment technologies. He has worked on most of the technology stacks.

He has hands on experience on UFT, LeanFT, Selenium and Appium. He has used testing frameworks like JUnit, TestNG, Cucumber with Selenium. He has also worked on Struts, Spring, Bootstratp, Angular JS.

His hobbies include travelling to new tourist places, watching basketball, cricket and learning latest technological stuff.

A special note of thanks to my Wife

I would like to dedicate this book to my lovely wife for loving me so much and helping me write this book. Without her support, this book would not have been a reality.

Who this book is for

This book is for automation engineers who want to learn Linux and Bash shell terminal.

The book starts with introduction of Linux and then dives into key concepts as mentioned below.

1. Linux installation
2. Understanding directory structures
3. Boot process, Run levels in Linux
4. Desktop Environments
5. Different shells
6. Internal and External Commands, Basic Linux Commands, Important files and directories in Linux
7. Environmental and Shell Variables, Command history in Linux
8. Character classes in Linux
9. Text editors
10. File and directory handling
11. Text Searching and processing
12. System commands
13. Processes and Jobs
14. Service command in Linux
15. Network commands
16. Managing Users and Groups
17. Other Popular commands
18. Standard streams and Redirection
19. Pipes
20. Package Managers in Linux
21. Shell scripting Introduction
22. Tools required for shell scripting

Table of Contents

1. Introduction – What is it? Why to learn?

Linux is an open source operating system.

Main features of Linux are given below.

1. Developed in C and assembly language
2. Open source
3. Widely used in servers (Since it is free!)
4. Android OS is built on the top of Linux kernel
5. POSIX compliant - POSIX is an IEEE standard for operating system compatibility.
6. Linux Kernel was developed by Linus Torvalds in 1991.

Linux is packaged in the form of distributions. The prominent distributions of Linux are -

1. UBUNTU
2. Debian
3. Linux Mint
4. Fedora
5. Redhat - Commercial
6. Suse - Commercial

In fact, anyone can distribute their own version of Linux since it is an open source software released under GPL.

Though Linux is not popular among dektop users, its use is gaining momentum due to new features being added in popular distributions like UBUNTU.

2. Linux installation – Distributions

So you have decided to learn Linux..As you know Linux comes in different distributions, you might get confused while selecting the distribution.

The most popular distributions are given below.

1. Ubuntu
2. Lubuntu
3. Mint
4. Debian
5. Fedora
6. Suse
7. Red Hat

If you want to install linux on your personal computer, you can go for Ubuntu. Lubuntu is the light version of Ubuntu. If you are planning to install linux on virtual box, you can go for Lubuntu since it needs less than 1 GB memory to run in a responsive manner.

You can download the iso (disc image file) from the official website and then install it on your machine as a standalone OS or on virtualbox or VMware Workstation.

3. Understanding directory structures

In this section, we will see how the directory structure is organized in Linux operating system.

The important directories and their significance are given below.

1. / - root directory
2. /home/ - parent directory of users
3. /etc - system configuration files are stored in this directory
4. /bin - executable programs like ls, date, time, cat...
5. /proc - stores the process related information
6. /root - home directory for the root user
7. /var - stores dynamic files and data
8. /tmp - stores temporary data of system and users
9. /opt - stores the files or data for optional or other installed programs on the system

Please note that apart from standard directories, you may have other directories in the tree based upon the distribution you are using.

4. Boot process, Run levels in Linux

Linux Boot process

In this section, we will see how the linux system boots. When we start the system, below sequence of events occur.

1. Read BIOS and see the boot device(CD ROM, USB or hard disk).
2. Try to locate the MBR (Master Boot Record) in boot device.
3. MBR contains the GRUB which stores the details of the kernels available for booting.
4. If there are multiple operating systems installed on your system, GRUB (also called as boot loader) displays the list of them and finally reads the selected kernel of the OS.
5. Kernel executes init process and then starts various other services.
6. Finally login prompt is displayed if the password is set for the user.

While executing above steps, below files are used in the process.

1. /boot/grub/grub.conf - stores details about kernels
2. /sbin/init - first process started in linux
3. /etc/inittab - defines run levels of the system
4. /etc/rc.d/rc0.d

Also note that init is the first process started by kernel. init process keeps running in the background as long as system is up and running. So it is also called as daemon process.

Run levels in Linux

A Linux system can be in specific run level. Linux system usually can have 7 run level (0-6).

0 run level is used to shut down the system.

6 run level is used to reboot the system.

Run levels 1 to 5 are used to start the system in single user or multi user mode and with or without networking.

We can use below command to check run level of the system.

```
$ runlevel
$ who -r
```

To know which processes will start in any of the run level, you can use below command.

```
$ chkconfig
```

You can use below command to shut down the system.

```
$ init 0
```

You can use below command to restart the system.

```
$ init 6
```

5. Desktop Environments

When you login to the linux system, the first graphical interface you see is the Desktop of your system.

There are different kinds of desktop environments in Linux as mentioned in below list.

1. GNOME
2. KDE
3. LXDE
4. LXQt

Most of these desktops come bundled with operating systems. For example if you are using lubuntu, lxde comes along with it. If you are using Kubuntu, KDE plasma dektop is the default dektop environment.

When you are in desktop mode, you may want to switch to terminal mode. You can use "Ctrl+Alt+F1" hot key to switch to terminal mode.To switch back to desktop mode, you can press Ctrl+Alt+F7 hot key.

6. Linux Shells

Shell is a utility which can be used to execute programs and interact with operating system. You can think of shell as the bridge between users and Operating system.

You can interact with operating system by 2 kinds of shells.

1. Command line shell - bash, zsh, C-shell etc
2. Graphical shell - GNOME, KDE etc

In linux, Command line shells can be further divided into 2 main categories.

1. Bourne shell - sh, bash(default shell program), ksh, zsh, ksh
2. C shell - csh

Command line shells run inside the program called as terminal.

You can use below command to see which shells are installed on your system.

```
cat /etc/shells
```

You can use below command to see your shell type.

```
echo $SHELL
```

6.1 BASH shell in Linux

BASH is the default shell in most of the Linux operating systems. To launch new shell terminal in Ubuntu, you can use CTRL+ALT+T hotkey. You can SHIFT+CTRL+N to create a new terminal window. You can use SHIFT+CTRL+N hotkey to start new terminal tab within existing window.

You can check what shell you are running by using below command.

```
echo $SHELL
```

If you see the output as /bin/bash, it means that you are using the BASH Shell.

To find out all commands starting with specific letter or letters, you can type the letter and press the TAB key twice.

Also you do not need to enter the full directory or file name. You can type first few characters of the file and then press tab key. BASH will auto complete the file name automatically provided it is able to identify the file uniquely.

For example - let us say we have 2 directories with name bigcities and bigcountries. Then to change the directory to bigcities, you can use below command.

```
cd bigc
```

and then press TAB key. Directory name will be auto-completed. But if type only "big" and then press TAB key, name will not be auto-completed because BASH does not find the unique directory name.

To exit the shell you can use below command

```
$ exit
```

You must know below things when working with BASH.

1. CTRL+c - This hotkey sends SIGINT singal (Interrupt signal) to the application. It is up to the application if it has to terminate itself.
2. CTRL+z - This hotkey sends SIGTSTP singal (Stop signal) to the foreground application. Application is sent to the background in suspended mode.
   You can view all application that are in background using jobs command.
3. CTRL+a - sends the cursor to the start of the command line.
4. CTRL+e - sends the cursor to the end of the command line.
5. CTRL+u - Cut the left portion of command from the cursor position.
6. CTRL+k - Cut the right portion of command from the cursor position.
7. CTRL+r - Search for the commands from command history and execute it.
8. ALT+. - Access the last argument of previous command on the command line.
9. CTRL+w - Delete one word from the command line

Some interesting stuff about running commands

We can run 2 commands one after another using below syntax.

```
cmd1  ;  cmd2
```

If you want to run second command only if first one is successful, you can use below syntax.

```
cmd1  &&  cmd2
```

If you want to run second command only if first one fails, you can use below syntax.

```
cmd1  ||  cmd2
```

You can run the command in background using below syntax.

```
cmd  &
```

7. Internal and External Commands

Internal and External Linux Commands

There are 2 types of Linux Commands.

1. Internal (Shell Built ins)
2. External

Internal commands are better than external commands from performance point of view
as shell does not have to fork new process to run internal commands (also called as built-ins).

You can find out if specific command is internal or external by executing below command.

```
$type <command-name>
```

If you get the output as command is "shell built-in", that means the command is internal otherwise it is external.

Here are the examples of Internal Commands

1. cd
2. echo
3. pwd

Here are the examples of External Commands

1. ls
2. dir

8. Basic Linux Commands

In this topic, we will look at some basic Linux command.

help command

We can list all available commands using below command

```
$ help
```

Getting help on specific command

We can get the manual of each command by using below command

```
$ man ls
```

compgen command

This command is very powerful and gives you lot of information about the system. This command can be executed with below options.

1. -a : This option is used to display all alias commands
2. -b : This option is used to display all internal commands (shell built-in commands)
3. -c : This option is used to display all commands (Internal and external)
4. -e : This option is used to display all exported shell variables

5. -g : This option is used to display all groups in the system
6. -j : This option is used to display all jobs in the system
7. -k : This option is used to display all BASH keywords
8. -s : This option is used to display list of all services running in the system
9. -v : This option is used to all shell variables (Environment as well as local shell variables)

You can use below command to see which shells are installed on your system.

```
cat /etc/shells
```

You can use chsh command to change your default shell

```
chsh -s /bin/bash
```

To find out your default shell, use below command

```
echo $SHELL
```

If you use -n option with echo command, it will not print new line.
printf command is similar to echo.

Various shells available are -
BASH, CSH, KSH, TCSH

We can find out location of the command by using below commands.

which ls - This command will display the location of binary file of ls command.

whereis ls - This command will display binary as well as other files like manuals related to ls command.

whatis ls - This command displays the information of given command in short line.

We can change the way command output is displayed using more and less commands

more is an old command. more command does not allow you to move forward and backward

less is latest command and we can move forward and backward using it
One you open a file using less command, following two keys are very helpful.

```
CTRL+F - forward one window
CTRL+B - backward one window
```

You can also use arrow keys to move back or forward by one line.
It is recommended to use less command.

history - This command shows all the commands in BASH history

Below command shows linux os details

```
uname -a
```

echo command in Linux

echo - print the text to standard output stream

For example - echo hello

Above command will print hello on the screen. Problem with above statement is that it will not preserve all white space characters. It will squeeze all adjacent white space characters in single white space character. It also remove the double quotes. Another problem is that BASH tries to expand the special characters. For example - command echo * will not print * but it will print all file and directories in current directory. To avoid these problems, you should wrap the message in double quotes.

For example - echo "hello"

To print the variables, you can use below command. The output will be /bin/bash

```
echo  "$SHELL"
```

To print value literally, you can use single quotes. The output will be $SHELL

```
echo  '$SHELL'
```

To execute command within echo, you will have to use back quotes ``

```
echo `ls`
```

cat - This is used to concatenate 2 or more files together and display the output to standard output screen.

For example - below command will display the contents of t1.txt followed by t2.txt

```
cat t1.txt t2.txt

clear - Clears the terminal
```

We can evaluate the expressions using expr command.
For example - below command will display the output as 4.

```
expr 1 + 3
```

"true" command does nothing. It just return the exit status as 0.

"false" command does nothing. It just return the exit status as 1.

Linux commands are case sensitive and usually in lower case. So ls and LS are not same commands.

9. Important files and directories in Linux System

Here is the list of important files and directories in Linux System

1. /proc/stat : This file stores current system information.
2. /proc/meminfo : This file shows Memory Information.
3. /proc/filesystems : This file stores file system information.
4. /proc/cpuinfo : This file stores CPU information.
5. /usr/sbin : This directory stores binaries required for system administration.
6. /etc/resolv.conf : This file store DNS information of the system.
7. /etc/passwd: This file stores user information like user id, default shell, directory of user etc.
8. /etc/group : This file stores information of all groups in the system.
9. /etc/hosts: This file stores the list of known hosts.
10. /etc/fstab : This file stores static file system information.
11. /etc/crontab : This file stores all cron jobs.
12. ~/.bashrc : This file contains script to be executed at the beginning of shell terminal.
13. ~/.profile : This file contains the script to be run for login shells.

14. ~/.bash_history : This file contains all history commands.
15. ~/.bash_logout: This file contains script which gets executed when shell exits.

10. Environmental and Shell Variables

Variables are key-value pairs which are used by different processes in Linux.

There are 3 types of variables.

1. Temporary local Shell variables (Only available in current shell)
2. Temporary Shell Environment variables (available in current shell, processes spawned by current shell, and child shells)
3. Permanent User Environment Variables (stored and exported in .bashrc, .bash_profile, .bash_login, .profile)
4. System environment permanent variables (stored in /etc/environment, /etc/profile, /etc/profile.d/, /etc/bash.bashrc)

Creating temporary local shell variables

To create local shell variable, you can execute below command. Here we are creating variables with name "var1" and it's value is "value1".

```
var1=value1
```

set command can be used to see all local variables as well as environment variables.

Creating temporary environment variables

To create Global shell variable, you can execute below command. This variable can be accessed in child processes and child shells.

```
export var1=value1
```

Below image shows how you can create your own variables and then convert them into global variables. In below example, we have created new variable called as "SAGAR" and assigned it the value as "Hello". This is a temporary variable (Also called as Session Variable). To convert it into temporary environment variable, we have used export command. Note that exported variables are only available in child processes. Also next time if you open terminal and view the content of any exported variables, you will see nothing. To make the change permanent, you have to put that variable in .bashrc file under your home directory.

```
bash-4.3$ SAGAR="Hello"
bash-4.3$ set | grep SAGAR
SAGAR=Hello
bash-4.3$ printenv | grep SAGAR
bash-4.3$ export SAGAR
bash-4.3$ printenv | grep SAGAR
SAGAR=Hello
bash-4.3$ SAGAR="Hello1"
bash-4.3$ printenv | grep SAGAR
SAGAR=Hello1
bash-4.3$ set | grep SAGAR
SAGAR=Hello1
```

Creating Environment Variables

Global shell variables can be accessed in child shells and processes. But the problem is that these variables will be erased as soon as we close current shell terminal. That's when environment variables come into picture.

To convert the exported global variables into environment variables, you need to store below command in .bashrc or your login profile file. So that every time you login or open the shell, those variables can be accessed

```
export var1=value1
```

This is called as user defined environment variables. But there are many built-in environment variables that you can access.

Here is the list of some of the system built-in environment variables.

```
echo $BASH  - displays the path of bash
shell.
echo $HOME - displays the home directory of
current user.
echo $OSTYPE - displays the OS type.
echo $SHELL - displays current shell type.
echo $PWD - displays present working
directory.
echo $PATH - displays contents of the PATH
variable.
```

Permanent User Environment Variables

You can view all the environment variables by using below command.

```
printenv
```

or you can also use "env" command to print the environment variables. Note that these command will not show local shell variables.

Sample output of above command is given below.

```
bash-4.3$ printenv
SCRIBACONF=/usr/local/scriba/etc/basic.conf
HOSTNAME=27f70a2aacc4
GNUSTEP_IS_FLATTENED=yes
TERM=xterm-256color
SMLROOT=/usr/local/smlnj/bin
GNUSTEP_LOCAL_ROOT=/usr/GNUstep/Local
GNUSTEP_HOST=x86_64-unknown-linux-gnu
JRE_HOME=/opt/jdk1.7.0_75/jre
LD_LIBRARY_PATH=/home/cg/root/GNUstep/Library/Libraries:/usr/GNU
ies:/usr/GNUstep/System/Library/Libraries:/usr/local/lib:/usr/li
GUILE_LOAD_PATH=/home/cg/root/GNUstep/Library/Libraries/Guile:/u
Libraries/Guile:/usr/GNUstep/System/Library/Libraries/Guile
GNUSTEP_MAKEFILES=/usr/GNUstep/System/Library/Makefiles
GNUSTEP_NETWORK_ROOT=/usr/GNUstep/Network
HAXE_STD_PATH=/usr/local/bin/std:/usr/local/bin/extra
GNUSTEP_FLATTENED=yes
GNUSTEP_HOST_OS=linux-gnu
GNUSTEP_HOST_VENDOR=unknown
PATH=/home/cg/root/GNUstep/Tools:/usr/GNUstep/Local/Tools:/usr/G
local/bin:/usr/bin:/usr/local/sbin:/usr/sbin:/home/webmaster/.lo
in:/usr/local/scriba/bin:/usr/local/smlnj/bin:/usr/local/bin/std
r/local/fantom/bin:/usr/local/dart/bin:/usr/bin:/usr/local/bin:/
/opt/mono/bin:/opt/mono/lib/mono/4.5:/usr/local/bin:.:/usr/libex
```

To view specific variable value, you can use any of the below commands.

1. echo $HOME
2. printenv HOME

Editing Environment Variables

You can edit the environment variables by using below command. Editing the variable is very simple. Just set the new value for the variable at command prompt. Remember that changes made to the environment variables within shell are temporary.

For example - If you want to change the variable called PWD, you can do it using below command.

```
PWD="new directory name"
```

Deleting the Environment Variables

You can delete the variables by using unset command.

```
unset  SAGAR
```

Special variables in Linux

1. $# - This displays total number of command line arguments.
2. $* and $@ - This displays all arguments to the shell.
3. $$ - This displays the process id of current shell.

4. $! - This displays the process id of the last background process started with & symbol.
5. $0, $1, $2 and so on - $0 is the name of the command running at the moment. $1 is the first argument to the command. $2 is the second argument to the command and so on.

Storing environment variables

You should store all environment variables in any of below files.

1. ~/.bashrc - This is user specific file. This file is sourced every time you open new bash shell.
2. ~/.bash_profile - This is user specific file.
3. ~/.bash_login - This is user specific file. Variables are initialized from this file at the start of login shell.

But you can also store the variables in below files. Variables in below files will be available in all applications (not only bash)

1. /etc/environment - Variables stored in this file are available across system and for every user. Also these variables will be available local as well remote sessions.
2. /etc/profile - Variables in this file will not be accessible for local login session.
3. /etc/bash.bashrc - Variables are available for local user sessions.

You can get more information about start up files using below command.

```
$ man bash
```

11. Command history in Linux

When you type commands in shell, all those commands are saved in history file in Linux. So next time, you can execute the commands in history using shortcuts. This saves your time.

You can set the history size using below syntax. Below command will instruct shell to save only 111 latest commands in the history.

```
$ set history=111
```

To display all commands in the history, you can use below syntax.

```
$ history
```

Here are some of the shortcuts to execute the commands in the history.

1. $!! - This is used to execute last command.
2. $!-n - This is used to execute second last command.
3. $!n - This is used to execute nth command in the list.

You should also remember below things when working with BASH.

1. !! - Execute last command
2. !xyz - Execute the command (starting with xyz) from the command history

3. !xyz:p - Print the command (starting with xyz) from the command history
4. !$ - Execute the last argument of previous command. Note that argument should be the command. For example let us say you execute below command.ls -a

   And then execute !$ command. Then bash will execute command "-a". But since it is not a valid command, you will get an error message saying -a : command not found.
5. !* - Execute the all arguments of previous command. Note that all arguments combined together should be a the commandFor example let us say you execute below command.

   ls -a -l

   And then execute !$ command. Then bash will execute command "-a -l". But since it is not a valid command, you will get an error message saying -a : command not found.
6. ^xyz^pqr - Run previous command replacing xyz with pqr. Note that only command string is replaced ..not the arguments

You can also erase and ignore duplicate commands by configuring below variables.

1. export HISTCONTROL=erasedups
2. export HISTCONTROL=ignoredups

To ignore the commands starting with space, you can use below command.

```
export HISTCONTROL=ignorespace
```

To clear history, you can use below command.

```
$ history -c
```

To disable history, you can use below command.

```
$ export HISTSIZE=0
```

12. Character classes in Linux

Here is the list of character classes in Linux. They are used in pattern matching.

1. [:alpha:] matches letters only.
2. [:digit:] matches numbers only.
3. [:alnum:] matches letters and numbers only.
4. [:xdigit:] matches hexadecimal numbers.
5. [:lower:] matches a-z.
6. [:upper:] matches A-Z.
7. [:blank:] matches a space or a tab.
8. [:space:] matches white space and horizontal tab.
9. [:cntrl:] matches control characters.
10. [:print:] Printable characters in the range of ASCII 32 - 126.

13. Text editors

Text editor is a program which can be used to create, modify or append the text files.

We can categorize the text editors in 2 types.

1. Console based
2. GUI based

Popular console based text editors in Linux are mentioned in below list.

1. vi/vim
2. nano

Popular GUI based text editors in Linux are mentioned in below list.

1. gVim
2. gedit

13.1 Vim Editor

In this topic, you will learn how to work with Vim editor in Linux.

Vim has below features.

1. Vim allows you to create,edit text files.
2. Vim is advanced version of Vi editor.
3. We can also compare files using vimdiff.
4. Vim supports syntax highlighting for C, C++, Python etc

To start the Vim from shell, just type "vim" command. You can also give the name of the file.

```
vim xyz
```

If you want to open file in read only mode, you can use below command.

```
vim -R abc.txt
```

There are 2 modes in vim.

1. Command mode
2. Insert mode

By default, you are in command mode. To go to insert mode, press i. Once you are in insert mode, you can edit the text file very easily. You can use backspace and delete keys just like how you use it in notepad in windows.

To go back to command mode, press escape.

In command mode, you can use below commands to perform various actions.

1. :w - This command will save your file. :w command will save the current file. If you want to save the current file in another file say f2, you can use command ":w f2". Note that f2 file will be created but vim will continue to hold original file in buffer. To work on new file, you will have to use command ":sav f2" instead of ":w f2".
2. :q - This command will exit the editor. ALternatively you can use :quit.
3. :wq - This command can be used to save and exit at the same time.

Linux – A Beginner's Guide

4. :q! - This command can be used to exit without saving the file.
5. v - command can be used to copy the selected text.
6. V - command can be used to copy entire line
7. d - command can be used to cut the text or entire line
8. y - command can be used to copy the text or line
9. p - command can be used to paste the text at cursor location

Errors in Vim

You may encounter below errors when working with vim. But you can easily avoid these errors by following basic instructions.

1. Press enter or type command to continue - This error comes when you don't use the proper command. For example if you use :!q command instead of :q!, you will get this kind of error.

2. readonly option is set (add! to override) - This error comes when you try to save the changes to read only file. For example If you have read only permission on a file and you change that file in vim, then you will not be allowed to write to that file. Note that vim allows you editing that file but does not allow you saving that file. You can make any file read-only by executing "chmod 0444 myfile" command.

38

3. No write since last change - This error comes when you try to quit without saving changes using :q command.

4. Not an editor command :W - This error comes when you are using capital W instead of small cap w.

13.2 nano editor

nano is a basic text editor in Linux.

Main features of nano are given below.

1. very easy and short learning curve
2. shortcuts to important actions are given at the bottom of editor
3. very easy for someone coming from windows background

The drawback of nano is that it does not provide syntax highlighting and many other features available in vim.

To start the nano editor from shell, you can execute below command.

```
nano filename
```

Then you can start editing the file. We do not have insert and command modes (available in vim) in nano.

Here are some of the shortcuts in nano.

1. Ctrl + o - To save the file you can use ctrl+o hotkey.
2. Ctrl + x - This hotkey is used to exit the nano editor.

3. Ctrl + w - This hotkey is used to find the text in a file in nano editor.

4. Ctrl + r - load the specified file in nano

5. Alt + k - Select the text

6. Ctrl + k - Cut the text

7. Ctrl + u - Paste the selected text

8. Alt + / - This hot key can be used to go to the end of file

9. Ctrl + a - This hot key can be used to go to the beginning of current line

10. Ctrl + e - This hot key can be used to go to the end of current line

11. Ctrl + c - shows current position of the cursor like line number, column number etc

12. Ctrl - (dash) - This command will let you jump to specific line number in a file

13. Ctrl + w - Allows you to find the text in a file. To find the next occurrence, you can use Alt + w command.

14. File and directory handling

14.1 Searching files and directories

We can search files (and directories) using 4 commands.

1. find
2. locate
3. whereis
4. which (only binaries)

find Command

Syntax of find command is given below.

```
$ find path_where_to_find nameOfFile
```

Examples -

Finding files by name

To find the files and directories with exact name, you can use below command.

```
find . -name "f1.txt"
```

To find the files and directories with containing specific word

```
find . -name "*xyz*"
```

To find only directories containing specific word, you can use below command

```
find . -name "*xyz*" -type d
```

To find only files containing specific word, you can use below command

```
find . -name "*xyz*" -type f
```

To find only files containing specific word, you can use below command

```
find . -name "*xyz*" -type f
```

To find all files and directories ending with .txt, you can use below command in Case Insensitive manner. Here -iname stands for case insensitive.

```
find . -iname "*.txt"
```

To find all files and directories with name f1 only in current directory (Not sub directories), you can use below command. Here "-maxdepth" indicates the directory level.

```
find . -maxdepth 1 -name "f1"
```

Operators in find command

1. find . -not -name "abc" : This command will search all files except with name "abc"
2. find . ! -name "abc": This command is same as above command.
3. find -name '*.php' -o -name '*.txt' : This command will find the files where name ends with ".php" or ".txt"

Finding file using regular expression

```
$ find ./ -regex '.*f1.*'
```

Finding file based on user or group

Below command will find the files and directories in current directory and sub-directories where the user of the file or directory is paul.

```
$ find . -user paul
```

Below command will find the files and directories in current directory and sub-directories where the group of the file or directory is dev.

```
$ find . -group dev
```

Finding file based on access (a), modification (m) and change(c) in attributes time

atime stands for files accessed in 24*N Hours (or in N days). Same applies to mtime and ctime.

amin stands for files accessed in N minutes. Same applies to mmin and cmin.

```
N can be prefixed with +, - or nothing.

+N means find the files before N

-N means find the files between N and now

N means find the files exactly on N
```

Examples -

Below command will find the files and directories in directory "mydir" and sub-directories where the files were modified between 10 minutes ago and now.

```
$ find ./mydir -mmin -10
```

Below command will find the files and directories in directory "mydir" and sub-directories where the files were modified on exactly 10th minute in the past.

```
find ./mydir -mmin 10
```

Below command will find the files and directories in directory "mydir" and sub-directories where the files were modified before 10th minute.

```
find ./mydir -mmin +10
```

Below command will find the files and directories in directory "mydir" and sub-directories where the files were modified between 20 and 40 days in the past.

```
find ./mydir -mtime +20 -mtime -40
```

Finding file based on permissions and attributes

1. find . -perm /a=x : This command will find files and directories with execute permission for current user.
2. find . -perm /u=r : This command will find files and directories with read only permission for current user.
3. find . -perm 0664 : This command will find files and directories with specific permission for current user.

Finding file based on size

1. find . -type f -size +20M : This command will find all files with size >= 20 MB
2. find . -empty : This command is used to find empty files and directories
3. find . -size +2M -size -5M : This command will find files between 2MB and 5MB

Performing bulk operation on files

We can also perform the operations on files found by "find" command using below syntax.

1. find . -type f -exec ls -l {} \;
2. find . -type f | xargs ls -l

Main difference between -exec option and xargs is that when you use -exec option, the specified command is executed for each file. So if find command finds 3 files, "ls" command is executed 3 times. But in case of xargs, "ls" command is executed only once. xargs will invoke "ls" command only once with names of the found files as arguments. So xargs is much faster as compared to -exec option.

locate Command
The syntax of the locate command is given below.

```
$ locate <fileName>
```

"locate" command searches for a file in the database called as mlocate (/var/lib/mlocate/mlocate.db). It is recommeded to update the database before using locate command.

You can use below command to update the mlocate database.

```
$ updatedb
```

whereis Command

The syntax of the whereis command is given below.

```
$ whereis fileName
```

which Command

The syntax of which command is given below. Note that fileName should be executable binary.

```
$ which fileName
```

14.2 Creating new files

We can create a file in Linux in many ways.

1. cat > myfile.txt : This command will accept the data from standard input and put it in "myfile.txt". Note that you will have to press the ctrl+c hot key to mark the end of input.
2. touch "myfile" : This command will create file if it does not exist.
3. printf "This will go in file " > "myfile"
4. echo "This will go in file " > "myfile"
5. You can create a file using output redirection operator (>). Output of any command is sent to new file.
6. nano/vi - You can also use any of the editors to create a new file

14.3 Viewing File Contents

You can use any of the below commands to view the file contents.

1. cat <file-name>
2. head <file-name>
3. tail <file-name>
4. tac <file-name> : This command displays file from bottom to top
5. less <file-name>
6. more <file-name>
7. awk '1' <file-name>
8. sed -n '1,$p' <file-name>
9. grep "." <file-name>
10. text editors like nano, pico, vi, emacs

14.4 File commands

In this topic, you will learn about various commands required for managing files and directories in Linux.

Displaying the contents of file

"cat" command is used to display the contents of file. "tac" command is also used to display contents of file but from bottom to top.

Here is the syntax of cat command.

```
$ cat <file-name>
```

To number the lines in the output, you can use below command.

```
$ cat -n <file-name>
```

"rev" command displays the file contents but each line is reversed.

Deleting entire data from a file

To make the file empty, we can use any of the below command.

1. : > file1

    >file1

2. cat /dev/null > file1
3. truncate -s 0 file1

Creating a directory using mkdir command

```
$ mkdir <directory-name>
```

Deleting a file or a directory using rm command

```
$ rm   <file-name-or-directory-name>
```

To delete the files recursively in a directory, you can use below command.

```
$ rm   -r <directory-name>
```

To prompt the user before deleting file, you can use below syntax.

```
$ rm -i <file-name>
```

Copying files using cp command

Here is the syntax of cp command.

```
cp <source-file> <destination-file>
```

If you want to preserve, attributes of file like mode, ownership etc, you can use below command.

```
$ cp -p <source-file> <destination-file>
```

If you want to copy files interactively, you can use below command. Before each copy operation, you will be asked for the permission.

```
$ cp -i <source-file> <destination-file>
```

Renaming and moving files using mv command

You can use below command to rename a file.

```
$ mv <old-file> <new-file>
```

You can use below command to move a file.

```
$ mv <source-file> <destination-file>
```

You can use below command to move files interactively.

```
$ mv -i <source-file> <destination-file>
```

You can use below command to move a files forcibly. If the destination file exists, it will be overwritten.

```
$ mv -f <source-file> <destination-file>
```

Listing files and directories using ls command.

"ls" command shows the list of file names in the directory. But if you want to know other details of the file like its size, permission etc, you can run below command.

```
$ ls -l
```

Here is the list of other ls Options

1. -a : This option is used to show all files including hidden ones.
2. -R : This option is used to list files recursively from sub-directories.
3. -r : This option is used to list files in reverse order.
4. -S : This option is used to sort the files by size.
5. -1 : This option is used to list files separated by new line character.
6. -m : This option is used to list files separated by coma (,)
7. -Q : This option is used to list files in double quotes (" ")

Understanding the output of ls -l command

Below image shows the sample output of ls command.

```
Sagar@Sagar-Windows10 ~
$ ls -l
total 90370
-rwxr-xr-x  1 Sagar Sagar      135 Nov  2 20:18 cities.sh
-rwxr-xr-x  1 Sagar Sagar 18188046 Jul  9 10:47 com.google.android.gm-17.apk
-rwxr-xr-x  1 Sagar Sagar 34404105 Jul  6 17:44 com.localeur.release1-1.apk
-rwxr-xr-x  1 Sagar Sagar 39637067 Jul  9 10:33 com.viber.voip-10.apk
drwxr-xr-x+ 1 Sagar Sagar        0 Nov  9 12:14 d1
drwxr-xr-x+ 1 Sagar Sagar        0 Nov  9 12:14 d2
drwxr-xr-x+ 1 Sagar Sagar        0 Nov  9 12:14 d3
-rw-r--r--  1 Sagar Sagar       27 Nov  9 15:35 hi
drwxr-xr-x+ 1 Sagar Sagar        0 Jul 10 10:13 node_modules
-rwxr-xr-x  1 Sagar Sagar   297978 Jul 17 17:52 SecCalculator2_ESS.apk
```

ls-command-output

First line shows total file system blocks required to store all files and sub directories in current directory. After that , there is a line for each file.

The 1st character in the each line can take any of the below value.

1. "-" means it is a regular file
2. "l" means it is a link file
3. "d" means it is a directory
4. "c" means it is a character device
5. "b" means it is a block device
6. "p" means it is a pipe
7. "C" means high performance file
8. "s" means socket file
9. "?" means other unknown file

After that permission attributes are listed for each file for owner, group and others. Then the count of number of hard links is displayed. After that owner and group of file is displayed. Then file size, access time and file name is displayed.

file command

"file" command is used to display the type of file (e.g. ASCII file, BZ2 file etc)

```
$ file <file-name>
```

Viewing file attributes using stat command

"stat" command is used to display file attributes.

```
Sagar@Sagar-Windows10 ~
$ stat hi
  File: 'hi'
  Size: 27            Blocks: 1          IO Block: 65536  regular file
Device: cc3b2616h/3426428438d   Inode: 371546969925891113  Links: 1
Access: (0644/-rw-r--r--)  Uid: (197610/   Sagar)  Gid: (197610/    Sagar)
Access: 2016-11-09 15:34:54.240732800 +1000
Modify: 2016-11-09 15:35:23.407926000 +1000
Change: 2016-11-09 15:35:23.407935800 +1000
 Birth: 2016-11-02 19:29:00.133507200 +1000
```

stat-command-in-linux

Changing attributes of file using touch command

"touch" command is used to change the file access and modification time.

"-a" option stands for access time.
"-m" option stands for modification time.

```
Sagar@Sagar-Windows10 ~
$ stat hi
  File: 'hi'
  Size: 27          Blocks: 1          IO Block: 65536  regular file
Device: cc3b2616h/3426428438d   Inode: 37154696925891113  Links: 1
Access: (0644/-rw-r--r--)  Uid: (197610/    Sagar)   Gid: (197610/    Sagar)
Access: 2016-11-02 19:29:00.133507200 +1000
Modify: 2016-11-02 19:29:00.134488700 +1000
Change: 2016-11-02 19:29:00.134488700 +1000
 Birth: 2016-11-02 19:29:00.133507200 +1000

Sagar@Sagar-Windows10 ~
$ touch -a hi

Sagar@Sagar-Windows10 ~
$ stat hi
  File: 'hi'
  Size: 27          Blocks: 1          IO Block: 65536  regular file
Device: cc3b2616h/3426428438d   Inode: 37154696925891113  Links: 1
Access: (0644/-rw-r--r--)  Uid: (197610/    Sagar)   Gid: (197610/    Sagar)
Access: 2016-11-09 15:34:54.240732800 +1000
Modify: 2016-11-02 19:29:00.134488700 +1000
Change: 2016-11-09 15:34:54.240348700 +1000
 Birth: 2016-11-02 19:29:00.133507200 +1000

Sagar@Sagar-Windows10 ~
$ touch -m hi

Sagar@Sagar-Windows10 ~
$ stat hi
  File: 'hi'
  Size: 27          Blocks: 1          IO Block: 65536  regular file
Device: cc3b2616h/3426428438d   Inode: 37154696925891113  Links: 1
Access: (0644/-rw-r--r--)  Uid: (197610/    Sagar)   Gid: (197610/    Sagar)
Access: 2016-11-09 15:34:54.240732800 +1000
Modify: 2016-11-09 15:35:23.407926000 +1000
Change: 2016-11-09 15:35:23.407935800 +1000
 Birth: 2016-11-02 19:29:00.133507200 +1000
```

touch-command-in-linux

Soft links and hard links to files

Link is nothing but the file pointing to another file. There are 2 types of links.

1. Soft Link - inode numbers are different. If you delete the original file, soft link file will fail.
2. Hard Link - inode numbers are same. Even if you delete the original file, hard link file will work.

54

You can use below syntax to create soft link.

```
ln -s <original-file-path> <link-file>
```

You can use below syntax to create hard link.

```
ln <original-file-path> <link-file>
```

pushd and popd commands

pushd and popd commands are used to switch between directories very easily.

pushd command pushes the directory on the top of stack and also changes directory.

For example - Below command will change the directory to "d1" and also push the "d1" to top of the directory stack.

```
pushd d1

Directory stack will look like  d1 ~
```

Note that "~" indicates that home directory is also pushed to stack by default. So right now we are in "d1"

Now let us say you want to change to directory to "d2"

```
pushd d2

Directory stack will look like  d2 d1 ~
```

If we pushed another directory - "d3", stack will look like d3 d2 d1 ~

Now suppose you wish to switch directory say d2, then use below command.

```
pushd +1
```

You can think of stack as an array with first value accessed at 0. Now we will be switched to "d2" and stack will look like d2 d1 ~ d3

To change to directory "d3", you can use below command.

```
pushd +3
```

"popd" command is used to remove the directory from stack.

14.5 File permissions and ownership

A file or directory can have below types of permission attributes.

1. Read (r)
2. Write (w)
3. Execute(e)

A file also belongs to specific owner and group.

For example - In below image, we have listed down the permissions of file "a.sh". As you can see permissions are displayed in below format.

```
rwxrwxrwx
```

Also note that paul is the owner of this file and group of this file is paul as welll. You might be wondering why we have 3 sets of permission (rwx-rwx-rwx) for same file. You should remember that First set of permissions are for the user (u) of the file. Second set of permissions are for the users in specific group (g) of the file. Third set of permissions are for all other users (o).

```
paul@linux:~$ ls -l a.sh
-rwxrwxrwx 1 paul paul 26 Mar 16 04:17 a.sh
```
file-permissions-in-linux

Now consider permissions for below file - abc.txt. You can notice that owner and group of this file has only read and write permission. While all other users have only read permission. So if any other user tries to write to this file or execute this file, he will encounter error saying permission denied.

```
paul@linux:~$ ls -l abc.txt
-rw-rw-r-- 1 paul paul 3748 Mar 15 16:27 abc.txt
```
file-permissions-user-group-others-in-linux

We can use 3 commands to manage the permissions of the file.

1. chmod - change the file permissions
2. chown - change the ownership of the file
3. chgrp - change the group of the file

chmod command in Linux

chmod command is used to change the permission of a file or directory.

There are 2 ways in which we can specify the permission attributes.

1. symbolic
2. numeric

Symbolic file permission

It is very easy to work with symbolic file permissions. Let us say you want to give write permission on abc.txt file to others(o), then you can use below syntax. Here o stands for others. + means we are adding permission. w means we are adding write permission.

```
chmod o+w abc.txt
```

If you want to remove write access from others, you can use below syntax. here - means we are removing permission.

```
chmod o-w abc.txt
```

Now let us say you want to add write permission for user of the file and at the same time remove execute permission for group. Then you can execute below command.

```
chmod u+w,g-x abc.txt
```

Numerical permissions of file

You can also use numerical representation in chmod
command. Below

NUMBER	PERMISSION
7	rwx
6	rw-
5	r-x
4	r--
3	-wx
2	-w-
1	--x
0	---

For example to give read/write/execute permission to user of the file and no permission to group and other users, you can use below syntax.

```
chmod 700 abc.txt
```

chown command in Linux

chown command is used to change the owner and group of a file. Here is the syntax of chown command

```
chown <new_user>:<new_group> file
```

For example -
To change owner to paul and group to dev for file "abc.txt", you can use below command.

chown paul:dev abc.txt

To change the owner and group of all files in a directory, you can use -R option.

```
chown -R paul:dev /home/project
```

chgrp command in Linux

chgrp command is used to change the group of a file. Here is the syntax of chgrp command.

```
chgrp <group_name> file
```

You can also change the group of files recursively using below syntax.

```
chgrp -R <group_name> directory
```

Note that you might need to execute the commands using sudo to avoid error saying operation not permitted.

14.6 WildCards (Globbing) in files

Wildcards are used to match multiple files.

For example -

abc* - Here * will match all files that start with abc

abc[pqr] - here square bracket will match any file that starts with abc and ends with p or q or r

abc? - here ? will match just single character. It will match all files that start with abc and end with any other character.

BASH will expand the file names using wild cards.

Difference between WildCards (Globbing) and Regular expressions

It is worth noting that even though wildcard characters are same as meta characters in regular expressions, they are completely different.

For example -

abc* - If used as wildcard, it will match all files starting with abc. But if used as regular expression, it will match ab, abc, abcccc etc.

14.7 File archiving and compression

We can use zip and tar commands to archive and compress the files in Linux.

Archiving and Compressing using zip command

You can use below command to zip file abc.txt into abc.zip

```
$ zip abc.zip abc.txt
```

You will get below error if you do not provide the .zip destination file.

```
zip error! nothing to do
```

To compress directory, you need to use -r option. It means zip files recursively.

Below command can be used to unzip the zipped files.

```
$ unzip abc.txt.zip
```

Below command will list the zipped files without extraction.

```
$ unzip -l abc.txt.zip
```

Compressing files using gzip command

gzip uses deflat algorithm to compress data.
Below command will compress the abc.txt file to abc.txt.gz

```
$ gzip abc.txt
```

To compress directory, you need to use -r option. It means zip files recursively.

To uncompress any .gz file, you can use below command. Note that gunzip is an alias for below command.

```
$ gzip -d <file-name>.gz
```

Note that zcat is an alias for below command.

```
$ gunzip -c <file-name>.gz
```

Compressing files using bzip2 command

bzip2 uses Burrows-Wheeler algorithm which is less fast as compared to gzip but it makes more compact files than gzip.

To compress the file using bzip2, you need to use below command.

```
$ bzip2 abc.txt
```

To compress directory, you need to use -r option. It means zip files recursively.

To uncompress any *.bz2 file, you can use below command.

```
bzip2 -d <file-name>.bz2
```

Compressing file using xz command

xz compression uses LZMA2 algorithm. Remember that 7zip also uses the same algorithm.

Below command can be used to compress file using xz utility

```
$ xz <file-name>
```

Below command can be used to list the details of compression

```
$ xz -l <file-name>.xz
```

Below command can be used to uncompress the .xz file.

```
$ xz -d <file-name>.xz
```

Archiving and Compressing using tar command

In below example we are using tar command to archive and compress mybig-direcotry using basic algorithm. Here -c stands for create new archive and -x stands for extract compressed files. f stands for file.

```
$ tar -cvf mytarball.tar mybig-direcotry
$ tar -xvf mytarball.tar
```

In below example we are using tar command to archive and compress mybig-direcotry using gz algorithm.

```
$ tar -czvf mytarball.tar.gz mybig-
direcotry
$ tar -xzvf mytarball.tar.gz
```

In below example we are using tar command to archive and compress mybig-direcotry using bz2 algorithm.

```
$ tar -cjvf mytarball.tar.bz2 mybig-
direcotry
$ tar -xjvf mytarball.tar.bz2
```

In below example we are using tar command to archive and compress mybig-direcotry using xz algorithm.

```
$ tar -cJvf mytarball.tar.xz mybig-
direcotry
$ tar -xJvf mytarball.tar.xz
```

14.8 Directory commands

Below is the list of directory commands in Linux.

1. mkdir - create a new directory
2. pwd - print present working directory
3. cd - change directory
4. cp - copy one directory from source to destination
5. mv - move directory from source to destination
6. rm - delete directory
7. ls - view directory and files
8. chmod - modify the file or directory permissions

9. chown - change the user and group ownership of the file

As you have noticed, most of these commands also apply to files. In fact, linux does not differentiate between files and directories.

14.9 xargs command in Linux

xargs command is used to execute the command with dynamic arguments. Same command is executed for each argument one by one.

Some commands in Linux fail with error message saying "argument list too long". We can use "xargs" command in such scenarios as command will be executed one one argument at a time.

In below example, find command finds out all files with name matching "hi*" and contents are displayed on standard output stream.

```
find -maxdepth 1 -type f -name "hi*" |
xargs cat
```

14.10 Comparing files

We can use below commands to compare files in Linux.

1. diff - Compare files line by line
2. comm - Compare 2 sorted files line by line
3. cmp - Compare 2 files byte by byte

diff command

"diff" command shows the difference between 2 files.

```
$ diff <file1Name> <file2Name>
```

15. Text Searching and processing

15.1 Searching patterns using grep command

grep command is used to search the pattern in input file or input string. Regular expressions are used to specify the pattern.

Here is the syntax of grep command.

```
grep <pattern> <filename>
```

To highlight the matches, you can set GREP_OPTIONS variable with below values.

```
export GREP_OPTIONS='--color=auto'
```

We can use below command to find the pattern "abc" in file f1.txt

```
grep "abc" f1.txt
```

To make the search case insensitive, you can use -i switch

```
grep -i "abc" f1.txt
```

To print the line number where match is found, you can use -n switch

```
grep -n "abc" f1.txt
```

To print matched line and 3 lines after it, you can use below command

```
grep -n -A 3 "abc" f1.txt
```

To search for the pattern in all files in current directory and all subdirectories, you can use below command.

```
grep -r "abc" *
```

To suppress the message saying directories can not be searched, you can use -s switch.

```
grep -r -s "abc" *
```

We can use below command to find all lines not matching the pattern "abc" in file f1.txt. Here -v stands for inverted search.

```
grep -v "abc" f1.txt
```

Some more options on grep are given below.

1. grep -w "abc" f1 : "-w" option can be used to search for words (not sub strings).
2. grep -A 2 "abc" f1 : "-A" option can be used to display n lines after match.
3. grep -B 2 "abc" f1 : "-B" option can be used to display n lines before match.
4. grep -C 2 "abc" f1 : "-C" option can be used to display n lines before and after match.

5. grep -e "term1" -e "term2" : "-e" option is used to search multiple patterns in a file.

6. grep -c "abc" f1 : "-c" option is used to print the matches count.

7. grep -l "abc" * : "-l" option shows files names that match the pattern. (Instead of matching lines)

8. grep -o "xyz.*" f1 : "-o" option is used to print only the matched pattern (instead of whole line)

9. grep -n "term" f1 : "-n" option is used to display matching line numbers

If grep command encounters any directory while trying to search a pattern, it gives warning message saying "xyz is a directory". If you want to suppress this message, you can use "-s" switch.

egrep command

egrep command is equivalent to "grep -E". This is also called as extended grep.

fgrep command

fgrep command is equivalent to "grep -F". This is also called as fast grep.

15.2 Translating the characters using tr command

tr command is used to translate the input into another form.

tr command allows you to do below things on given data.

1. Replace the characters from given string with other set of characters.
2. Delete specific characters from the input string.
3. Squeeze the occurrences of specific character.

Here are the examples of tr command.

You can use below command to convert all upper case characters from the file to lower case.

```
cat myfile | tr [:upper:] [:lower:]
```

Another way to do same thing is by specifying the range of characters.

```
cat myfile | tr [A-Z] [a-z]
```

If you want to remove specific set of characters, you can use below command. Here "-d" stands for delete.

```
cat myfile | tr -d [A-C]
```

To remove spaces, you can use below command.

```
cat myfile | tr -d [:space:]
```

To remove all digits, you can use below command.

```
cat myfile | tr -d [:digit:]
```

To complement the output, you can use below command. In below example, everything except digits will be deleted from the file. Here "-c" option stands for complement.

```
cat myfile | tr -cd [:digit:]
```

To remove repeating occurrences of a character, you can use below command. Below command will replace all repeating occurrences of a by single character - a. Here "-s" stands for squeeze.

```
cat myfile | tr -s [a]
```

15.3 Extracting data using cut command

cut command allows you to extract specific portion of a line in a file.

Examples of cut command.

1. cat /etc/passwd | cut -d: -f1 - This command will display first column from the file /etc/passwd. Here f stands for field. d stands for delimiter.
2. cat /etc/passwd | cut -d: -f1,2 - This command will display first 2 columns from the file /etc/passwd.
3. cut -c2 <filename> : This command will extract and show second character from each line of a file
4. cut -c1-4 <filename> : This command will extract and show first 4 characters from each line of a file

5. cut -c4- <filename> : This command will extract and show all characters starting from 4th character from each line of a file
6. cut -d':' -s -f1 <filename> : This command will not display line of there is no delimiter found in the line. "-s" stands for suppress.
7. cut -d':' --complement -s -f1 <filename> : This command will complement the output. That means it will display all fields from the lines except field 1.
8. cut -d':' -s -f1,2 --output-delimiter='@' <filename> : This command will display different delimiter in output.

15.4 Stream editing using sed command

sed stands for stream editor. We can extract data from files or streams as well as edit the stream contents.

Here are some of the examples on sed command.

1. sed '1d' f1.txt - This command can be used to delete line number 1 from file f1.txt
2. sed '/^a/d' f1.txt -This command can be used to delete the lines starting with a
3. sed -n '1,4p' f1.txt - This command can be used to print lines 1,2,3 and 4
4. sed -n '/abc/p' f1.txt - This command can be used to print lines matching the pattern specified between / /
5. sed 's/abc/xyz/gi f1.txt - This command can be used to substitute the occurrences of abc by xyz in file f1.txt. Here s stands for substitute, g stands for

global (all occurrences) and i stands for case-insensitive replacement.

6. sed '1s/abc/xyz/g' f1.txt - This command is similar to above. The difference is that it will do case sensitive replacement in line number 1 only.

15.5 Data extraction and reporting using awk command

awk is a very powerful tool in Linux. awk allows you to do all things that can be done using grep, sed commands.

awk assumes the file as a database table. Each line is considered as a row and columns are separated by space. By default, space is used as a delimiter seperating columns. but you can mention different delimiter (field separator) by using FS option. Value in the first column can be accessed using $1, Value in the second column can be accessed using $2 and so on. Entire line (record) can be accessed using $0.

Below examples will help you understand how it work.

1. awk 'BEGIN{FS=":"} {print $1}' f1.txt - This command will print first column from the file f1.txt. Note that we have specified ":" as the field separator.

2. awk 'BEGIN{FS=":"} $1=='abc' {print $0}' f1.txt - This command will print only those lines from f1.txt where the value of first column is "abc"

3. awk 'BEGIN{FS=":"} $1!='abc' {print $0}' f1.txt - This command will print only those lines from f1.txt where the value of first column is not "abc"

4. awk '/abc/{print $1}' f1.txt - This command will print the first column from the file f1.txt where that lines matches the pattern "abc". Note that you can give the regular expressions in the pattern.

5. awk '!/abc/{print $1}' f1.txt - This command will print the first column from the file f1.txt where lines do not match the pattern "abc".

6. awk 'NR==7,NR==9' f1.txt - This command will print lines 7 and 9 from file f1.txt

Replacing the text using awk command

You can use below syntax to replace the pattern using awk.

```
$ awk
'{gsub(/pattern/,"replacement")}' <file-
name>
```

15.6 Sorting the file or string input

You can use sort command to sort the contents of a file or input string.

Sorting in acending order

For example - to sort the lines in a myfile in ascending order, you can use below command.

```
sort myfile
```

Sorting in descending order

To sort the lines in a myfile in descending order, you can use below command.

```
sort -r myfile
```

15.7 uniq command in Linux

uniq command is used to find only unique lines in a file.

1. uniq <file-name> : This command will display only unique lines in the file. Note that only adjacent duplicate lines are removed. To remove all duplicates, you can sort the contents of file and then pipe the output to uniq command.

2. uniq -c <file-name> : Here -c stands for count. It displays the count of occurences of each line.

3. uniq -d <file-name>: Here -d stands for duplicate. It displays the duplicate lines once for each set of duplicate occurence.

4. uniq -D <file-name> : It displays all occurrences of duplicate lines.

5. uniq -u <file-name> : It displays only unique line.

6. uniq -c -w 4 <file-name> :Use first 4 chars for checking uniqueness

7. uniq -D -s 4 <file-name> : avoid comparing first 4 chars

8. uniq -D -f 4 <file-name> : avoid compaing first 4 words

15.8 Difference between grep, tr, cut, sed and awk commands

1. grep can only shows the lines matching pattern. You can not transform the output.
2. tr command is used to replace the characters with other set of characters. Remember that sed works at pattern level.
3. cut command is used to extract characters, fields from a file. We can also specify the delimiter that separate the columns. Even though we can achieve same thing using sed command, it is recommended to use cut command for simplicity.
4. sed command is super set of grep, tr and cut command. Additionally it can transform output. sed is mainly used for extraction and substitution.
5. awk is a super set of sed. awk supports programming. awk is mainly used when the data is in the table format. It also allows to delete matching lines
   We can use programming constructs like for loop and conditions

16. System commands

16.1 System and Hardware commands

Below is the list of commands to get information about system and hardware.

1. free - used to display memory information
2. cat /proc/meminfo - memory information
3. fdisk - hard drive partition information
4. du - prints information about the disk usage
5. df - information about free disk space in given directory
6. lscpu - details about cpu
7. cat /proc/cpuinfo - cpu information
8. uname -a - Prints details of the operating system
9. last reboot - prints the time when system was last time rebooted
10. init 0/ shutdown -h - shutdown the system
11. reboot/init 6/ shutdown -r now - command to restart the system

uptime command

uptime command is used to display current time, the duration of time for which system is running, how many users are currently logged into the system. It also displays the average load on the system.

shutdown command

shutdown command is used to shut down the system.
Here -h means halt.

```
$ shutdown -h now
```

If you want to shut down the system after 5 minutes, you
can use below command.

```
# shutdown -h +5
```

If you want to reboot the system, you can use below
command. Here -r means reboot.

```
# shutdown -r now
```

16.2 Hard disk and memory space commands

Here is the list of hard disk and file system commands in
Linux.

mount and unmount command

mount command is used to mount the file system in Linux.
For example if you want to access the files from USB drive,
you will have to first mount the file system from USB drive
in the Linux System.

Below example shows how to mount a file system on
specific directory.

```
$ mount <file-system> <mount-directory>
```

You can also modify "/etc/fstab" file to mount the file system. "fstab" stands for file system table. This file contains entries for all mounted file systems.

df command

"df" command stands for disk free. As the name indicates, it displays how much space is used by specific file system. It also shows how much space is available on specific file system.

To display the size in human readable format (MG,GB,TB etc), you can use below command.

```
df -h
```

du command

"du" stands for disk usage. This command is used to display the space occupied by specific file or a directory.

For example - below command will display the space occupied by /etc directory and all files and sub-directories in it. "-h" will display the usage in human readable format (MB, GB,TB etc) and "-c" will display the total usage in the end.

```
du -hc /etc
```

Finding the size of each directory as well as file

```
$ du -ah
```

Finding the size of entire directory

```
$ du -sh
```

Finding the size of all files and directories in only current directory

```
$ du -ah -maxd 1
```

free command

free command is used to show the details of RAM in Linux. By default RAM is displayed in KB. But you can use below commands to show the RAM in MB, GB, TB etc.

```
free -m
free -g
free -t
```

quota command in Linux

quota command is used to manage the disk quota of an user or group.

Assume that you set up 15 GB as hard limit quota and 14 GB as soft limit quota with grace period as 10.
Hard limit - With 15 GB as hard limit quota, user will not be allowed to store any more files after 15 GB space is used.

Soft limit - With 14 GB as soft limit quota, user will be given warning messages after disk usage exceeds 14 GB

Grace period - Grace period allows you to store files even though you have crossed hard limit.

Getting disk information of the system

You can use lshw command to get disk information. As you can see there are 2 types of disks attached to the system - /dev/cdrom (DVD reader) and /dev/sda (ATA Disk)

```
paul@paul-VirtualBox:~$ sudo lshw -class disk
  *-cdrom
        description: DVD reader
        physical id: 0.0.0
        bus info: scsi@0:0.0.0
        logical name: /dev/cdrom
        logical name: /dev/sr0
        capabilities: audio dvd
        configuration: status=nodisc
  *-disk
        description: ATA Disk
        product: VBOX HARDDISK
        physical id: 0.0.0
        bus info: scsi@2:0.0.0
        logical name: /dev/sda
        version: 1.0
        serial: VBb72c3738-019763b9
        size: 8GiB (8589MB)
        capabilities: partitioned partitioned:dos
        configuration: ansiversion=5 sectorsize=512 signature=0004c60f
```

lshw-command-to-get-disk-information

You can use lsblk command to display the block devices and mount points. You can use fdisk command to manage the partitions of specific disk.

```
paul@paul-VirtualBox:~$ lsblk
NAME    MAJ:MIN RM    SIZE RO TYPE MOUNTPOINT
sda       8:0    0      8G  0 disk
├─sda1    8:1    0    6.3G  0 part /
├─sda2    8:2    0      1K  0 part
└─sda5    8:5    0    1.7G  0 part [SWAP]
sr0      11:0    1   1024M  0 rom
paul@paul-VirtualBox:~$ sudo fdisk -l /dev/sda

Disk /dev/sda: 8589 MB, 8589934592 bytes
255 heads, 63 sectors/track, 1044 cylinders, total 16777216 sectors
Units = sectors of 1 * 512 = 512 bytes
Sector size (logical/physical): 512 bytes / 512 bytes
I/O size (minimum/optimal): 512 bytes / 512 bytes
Disk identifier: 0x0004c60f

   Device Boot      Start         End      Blocks   Id  System
/dev/sda1   *        2048    13201407     6599680   83  Linux
/dev/sda2        13203454    16775167     1785857    5  Extended
/dev/sda5        13203456    16775167     1785856   82  Linux swap / Solaris
```

disk-and-partitions

17. Processes and Jobs

17.1 Working with Processes

A process is nothing but a binary file that is currently executing (running). For example - When you execute ls command in Linux, the /bin/ls binary starts running. Every process has a parent process associated with it except the init process. When you execute any command in shell, the process that is created is a child process of a shell and a shell process is the parent of that process.

You can find the process id of shell by executing below command.

```
echo $$
```

Here list of commands related to processes in Linux.

1. ps - list the processes
2. top - more detailed information about the processes
3. kill pid - kills the process by id
4. killall processname - kills process by name
5. pstree command - shows the process tree

ps command in Linux

ps command lists down the processes started in current shell.

```
ps -f
```

To list down all processes of specific user, you can use below syntax.

```
ps -u <User_Name>
```

To list down all processes in a system, you can use below command.

```
ps -aux
```

top command in Linux

top command shows all processes in the system. It also shows cpu usage, memory usage, status of process, user of process etc.

kill command in Linux

kill command terminates the process by id. Below command will kill process with id 1233

```
kill -9 1233
```

here -9 means kill forcefully. Terminate signal is sent to the process. To view all signals, you can use below command.

```
kill -1
```

killall command in Linux

killall command terminates the process by name. Below command will kill all nano processes.

```
killall -9 nano
```

pstree command in Linux

pstree command shows the process tree of the system. We can easily find the parent and child of each process using pstree.

17.2 Managing Jobs

A job is a conceptual thing in Linux. With Job you can manage your own processes and send them in background and foreground.

A job can be sent in background in 2 ways.

1. using CTRL+z shorcut key. In this case, job is in suspended mode.
2. using & at the end of the command in shell. In this case, job is in running status in the background

To view all jobs in the background, you can use "jobs" command.

To get the job in foreground, you need to use "fg" command. This will get the most recent background job to the foreground.

But you can also get specific job to the foreground using below command.

```
fg %JOB_NUMBER
```

You can kill the job using below syntax.

```
kill %JOB_NUMBER
```

bg command can be used to resume suspended jobs in the background.

Main purpose of sending the job to background is that you can work on multiple jobs at the same time and you do not need to wait for the job to finish before starting new one.

You can use "disown" command to remove specific job from the list of jobs.

"wait" command is used to wait until background jobs have finished.

"suspend" command has the same effect as pressing hotkey "ctrl+z"

17.3 Working with cron jobs

cron is used to schedule the jobs in Linux. It allows you do below things.

1. Add the job in crontab for specific user
2. Remove the job in crontab
3. View history of cron jobs

Adding new cron job

You can add cron job using below command.

```
crontab -e
```

Then you need to add the jobs using below syntax.

```
minute hour dayOfMonth month dayOfWeek
<command>
```

For example - below command will schedule a cron job to run after every 20 minutes.

```
*/20 * * * * /home/myjob.sh
```

View cron jobs

Below command will list all cron jobs of current user.

```
$ crontab -l
```

Below command will list all cron jobs of given user.

```
$ crontab -u <user-name> -l
```

Removing cron jobs

Below command will remove all cron jobs of current user.

```
$ crontab -r
```

18. Service command in Linux

service command is used to run System V init script and daemon processes.

Here is the general syntax of service command.

```
service <scritp-name> command
```

You can use below command to see the status of all the services.

```
$ service --status-all
```

You can use below command to restart any service.

```
$ service <service-name> restart
```

You can use below command to stop any service.

```
$ service <service-name> stop
```

You can use below command to start any service.

```
$ service <service-name> start
```

List of well known services or daemons in Linux system

1. crond - cron scheduler
2. dhcpd - dynamic host configuration protocol manager
3. ftpd - ftp server daemon
4. httpd - http web server daemon
5. mysql - mysql server daemon
6. smtpd - mail protocol daemon
7. sshd - ssh server daemon
8. syslogd - system logging daemon

19. Network commands

Network commands are very helpful in getting information on network interfaces, IP addresses, physical addresses, network connections, domain look up and troubleshooting network issues.

Here is the list of network commands in Linux.

curl command in Linux

curl command allows you to work with applications using HTTP, FTP, FTPS, HTTPS, SCP, SFTP, TFTP, TELNET, DICT, LDAP, LDAPS, FILE, POP3, IMAP, SMTP, RTMP and RTSP protocols. For example - If you want to download any file from the web server, you can use below command.

```
$ curl www.softpost.org
```

If curl is not installed on your Ubuntu machine, you can install it using below command.

```
$ sudo apt-get install curl
```

Here is the list of curl commands.

1. $ curl www.softpost.org -> This command will download the home page of www.softpost.org and display it on standard output.
2. $ curl -o index.html www.softpost.org -> If you want to save the file instead of viewing it on console, you can use -o option and provide the file

name where you want to save downloaded file. Here -o stands for output.

3. $ curl -O www.example.com/example.html -> If you want to save the downloaded file with same name as url, you can use -O option.
4. $ curl https://securesite.com/login.html
5. $ curl --insecure https://self-signed-cert.com/login.html

wget command in Linux

wget command is just like curl. Main difference is that wget command supports only HTTP, HTTPS and FTP protocols. Also curl is more widely used than wget. wget can get the urls recursively.

Here is the list of wget commands.

1. $ wget www.softpost.org -> This command will download the home page of www.softpost.org and display it on standard output.
2. $ wget -o index.html www.softpost.org -> If you want to save the file instead of viewing it on console, you can use -o option and provide the file name where you want to save downloaded file. Here -o stands for output.
3. $ wget --input url-list.txt -> This command can be used to download multiple urls specified in url-list.txt file.

ping command in Linux

ping command is used to check the connection with other host

```
$ ping <host-name>
```

ping command sends the packets to given host indefinitely. If you want to restrict the packets to be sent to the host, you can use below command. Here ping command will send only 4 packets to host.

```
$ ping -c 4 <host-name>
```

ifconfig command in Linux

ifconfig command shows the ip address and physical address of each network interface on the host.

```
$ ifconfig -a
```

Below image shows the sample output of ifconfig command. The number next to HWaddr is the physical address of network interface. The number next to inet addr is the IP address of network interface.

```
paul@linux:~$ ifconfig -a
enp0s3    Link encap:Ethernet  HWaddr 08:00:27:91:69:cf
          inet addr:10.0.2.15  Bcast:10.0.2.255  Mask:255.255.255.0
     I    inet6 addr: fe80::a00:27ff:fe91:69cf/64 Scope:Link
          UP BROADCAST RUNNING MULTICAST  MTU:1500  Metric:1
          RX packets:1121 errors:0 dropped:0 overruns:0 frame:0
          TX packets:805 errors:0 dropped:0 overruns:0 carrier:0
          collisions:0 txqueuelen:1000
          RX bytes:675370 (675.3 KB)  TX bytes:70624 (70.6 KB)

lo        Link encap:Local Loopback
          inet addr:127.0.0.1  Mask:255.0.0.0
          inet6 addr: ::1/128 Scope:Host
          UP LOOPBACK RUNNING  MTU:65536  Metric:1
          RX packets:964 errors:0 dropped:0 overruns:0 frame:0
          TX packets:964 errors:0 dropped:0 overruns:0 carrier:0
          collisions:0 txqueuelen:0
          RX bytes:70275 (70.2 KB)  TX bytes:70275 (70.2 KB)
```

ifconfig-output

hostname command in Linux

$ hostname - This command can be used to print or set system name.

To change the name of your system, you will have to use below command.

```
$ hostname <new-host-name>
```

Also note that changes are temporary. To make the changes permanent, you will have to edit /etc/hostname file with the new host name.

dig/host/nslookup command in Linux

dig command is used for getting DNS information of domain name

```
$ dig www.softpost.org
```

Here is the sample output of dig command.

```
paul@linux:~$ dig www.softpost.org

; <<>> DiG 9.9.5-11ubuntu1.2-Ubuntu <<>> www.softpost.org
;; global options: +cmd
;; Got answer:
;; ->>HEADER<<- opcode: QUERY, status: NOERROR, id: 26289
;; flags: qr rd ra; QUERY: 1, ANSWER: 2, AUTHORITY: 0, ADDITIONAL: 1

;; OPT PSEUDOSECTION:
; EDNS: version: 0, flags:; udp: 4096
;; QUESTION SECTION:
;www.softpost.org.              IN      A

;; ANSWER SECTION:
www.softpost.org.       2827    IN      CNAME   softpost.org.
softpost.org.           600     IN      A       166.62.28.97

;; Query time: 252 msec
;; SERVER: 127.0.1.1#53(127.0.1.1)
;; WHEN: Wed Mar 16 07:41:53 AEDT 2016
;; MSG SIZE  rcvd: 75
```

dig-command-in-linux

host and nslookup commands also provide similar information.

traceroute command in Linux

traceroute command is used to trace the route to Host.

```
$ traceroute www.softpost.org
```

If this command is not available in your Ubuntu system, you can use below command to install it.

```
$ sudo apt-get install traceroute
```

netstat command in Linux

netstat stands for network statistics. This command shows all network connections as well as network interface information.

To know about all tcp and udp connections, you can use below command. Here -t stands for TCP connection. -u stands for UDP connections.

```
$ netstat -tu
```

You can use below command to know all network connections on your system.

```
$ netstat -a
```

lsof command in Linux

Below command can be used to display the list of all open files including the ones used by network connections.

```
$ sudo lsof
```

To list only TCP and UDP connections, you can use below commands

```
$ lsof -i tcp

$ lsof -i udp
```

To list processes listening on specific port say 80, you can use below command.

```
lsof -i :80
```

ftp command in Linux

ftp command allows you to upload, download, manage files on FTP server

To connect to any server, type below command.

```
$ ftp <server-name>
```

Once the connection is established, you will have to enter user id and password.

Once you log in successfully, you can issue below commands.

1. put filename - Upload a file to the server
2. get filename - Download a file from the server
3. mput *.txt - Put multiple files ending with .txt on the server
4. mget *.txt - Get multiple files ending with .txt from the server
5. ls - Get a list of files in the current directory
6. cd - Change directory
7. quit - Close your ftp session

telnet command in Linux

telnet command can be used to manage the compute remotely. It is less secure as compared to ssh command. Data is transferred in plain text.

ssh command in Linux

ssh stands for Secure Shell Protocol. You can remotely login to computer and execute the commands using ssh command. Data is encrypted before transmission.

Below command will show ssh version you are using.

```
$ ssh -V
```

route/arp command in Linux

route command shows the kernel routing table. Here is the sample output.

route-command-in-linux

arp stands for address resolution protocol. arp command shows all ARP entries in the system.

20. Managing Users and Groups

Linux is a multi-user operating system. It means that many user can work on the system simultaneously.

You can find out user information from /etc/passwd file.

Each Linux user should belong to a specific group.

You can find out groups information from /etc/group file.

Here is the snapshot of typical passwd and group file in Linux.

```
paul@linux:/home$ cat /etc/passwd
root:x:0:0:root:/root:/bin/bash
daemon:x:1:1:daemon:/usr/sbin:/usr/sbin/nologin
bin:x:2:2:bin:/bin:/usr/sbin/nologin
sys:x:3:3:sys:/dev:/usr/sbin/nologin
sync:x:4:65534:sync:/bin:/bin/sync
games:x:5:60:games:/usr/games:/usr/sbin/nologin
man:x:6:12:man:/var/cache/man:/usr/sbin/nologin
lp:x:7:7:lp:/var/spool/lpd:/usr/sbin/nologin
mail:x:8:8:mail:/var/mail:/usr/sbin/nologin
news:x:9:9:news:/var/spool/news:/usr/sbin/nologin
uucp:x:10:10:uucp:/var/spool/uucp:/usr/sbin/nologin
proxy:x:13:13:proxy:/bin:/usr/sbin/nologin
www-data:x:33:33:www-data:/var/www:/usr/sbin/nologin
backup:x:34:34:backup:/var/backups:/usr/sbin/nologin
list:x:38:38:Mailing List Manager:/var/list:/usr/sbin/nologin
irc:x:39:39:ircd:/var/run/ircd:/usr/sbin/nologin
```

passwd-file-contents

Each line in passwd file contains below information.

```
<username>:x:<userid>:<groupid>:<group_name
>:<home_directory>:<shell>
```

```
paul@linux:/home$ cat /etc/group
root:x:0:
daemon:x:1:
bin:x:2:
sys:x:3:
adm:x:4:syslog
tty:x:5:
disk:x:6:
lp:x:7:
mail:x:8:
news:x:9:
uucp:x:10:
man:x:12:
proxy:x:13:
kmem:x:15:
dialout:x:20:
fax:x:21:
voice:x:22:
cdrom:x:24:
```

group-file-in-linux

Each line in group file contains below information.

```
<groupname>:x:<groupid>
```

Below is the list of commands to manage users and groups in linux system.

1. useradd - add new user into the system
2. userdel - delete the specific user from the system
3. usermod - modify the user details
4. groupadd - add new group in the system
5. groupdel - delete specific group from the system

102

6. groupmod - modify the group details
7. passwd - change or set the password for given user.
8. finger user - Prints details about the user. Please note that you will to install finger package for this.
9. whoami - gives name of the user currently logged into the system
10. id - shows the user id, group id and group details for given user.

Setting up new user in Linux

You can create new user and set password for that user using 2 commands below. Below commands will create new user - "shaun"

```
sudo  useradd  shaun
sudo  passwd  shaun
```

Modifying user in Linux

You can modify user using usermod command. This command has many options that allow you to update the user.

1. usermod -d /home/newdir/ shaun -> New home directory for the user shaun
2. usermod -e 2017-12-30 shaun -> Set the expiry date for the user shaun
3. usermod -g newg shaun -> change the primary group of user shaun

4. usermod -aG secondaryg shaun -> append new group to user shaun
5. usermod -l mark shaun -> change login name of shaun to mark
6. usermod -L shaun -> lock user shaun
7. usermod -U shaun -> unlock user shaun
8. usermod -d /var/shaun/ -m shaun ->move home directory of shaun to new location
9. usermod -s /bin/sh shaun -> Change the default shell of user shaun
10. usermod -u 777 shaun -> Change the user id of shaun

You can also use multiple options in single line.

1. usermod -d /home/kk/ -s /bin/bash -e 2018-02-22 -c "This is abc" -u 4 -aG g1 shaun
2. usermod -u 111 -g 444 shaun

If you want to view the expiry date of user account, you can use below command.

```
chage  -l  shaun
```

Note that you can change the account expiry details using chage command as well. For example, if you want to change the account expiry of user shaun, you can use below command.

```
chage  shaun
```

Deleting the user using userdel command in Linux

You can delete a user using below command.

```
sudo userdel <username>
```

passwd command in Linux

When you execute passwd command, you will have to enter current password. If you want to change the password for other user, you can use below command. Note that you should be a root user to be able to change password of other users.

```
passwd <username>
```

A root user can also disable the password of other users using below command.

```
passwd -d <username>
```

If you want to change the passwords of multiple users at the same time, you can use below command followed by list of user name and their passwords.

```
chpasswd

<username>:<password>
```

id command in Linux

id command will display your user id, group id and the groups you belong to. If you want to see other user details you can use below syntax.

```
id <username>
```

group commands in Linux

You can use below commands to manage groups in Linux.

To add new group say "g1", you can use below command.

```
sudo groupadd g1
```

To rename the group from say "g1" to "newg1", you can use below command.

```
groupmod -n newg1 g1
```

To change the id of group, you can use below command. Here we are changing the id of group g1 to 1010

```
groupmod -g 1010 g1
```

To delete the group say "newg1", you can use below command.

```
sudo groupdel newg1
```

<u>Switching user accounts</u>

"su" command is used to switch user account.
Switch to a different user account using su command.
Super user can switch to any other user without entering their password.

sudo is similar command but only allows execution of one command at a time with special privileges.

21. Other Popular commands

Below is the list of popular linux commands.

1. man - prints manual page of the command
2. whereis - prints the location of command
3. which - prints the location of the command
4. type - prints the location of command
5. echo - prints the string, variable or file
6. mail - used to send an email
7. logout - log off from the system
8. date - prints system time stamp
9. cal - shows the calendar

zdump command

zdump command is used to display time in different time zone. For example - If you want to see the time in GMT, you can use below command.

```
zdump  GMT
```

dirname command

dirname command is used to get the name of directory in which file is stored. For example if the full path of file is /usr/home/f1.txt, then dirname will be /usr/home

basename command

basename command is used to get only main name of file. For example if the full path of file is /usr/home/f1.txt, then basename will be f1.txt

---

sleep command

sleep command is used to wait for fixed amount of seconds. For example to sleep for 2 seconds, use below syntax.

```
sleep 2
```

22. Standard streams and Redirection

In linux, we have 3 standard streams.

1. Standard input stream - 0 - Keyboard
2. Standard output stream - 1 - Shell terminal display
3. Standard error stream - 2 - Shell terminal display

When we type any characters from the keyboard, it goes into the standard input stream. When program executes and displays output, it is pushed into the output stream (Terminal Display) . Any error information is pushed into the error stream (Terminal Display).

But we don't want input or output to go into standard stream at all times. For example - input required for the program may be available in the file. So instead of reading from the keyboard(standard input stream - 0), we can read it from file itself. Similarly, output generated by the program may be redirected to file stream or any other stream instead of standard output stream (1 - Terminal Display).

We have below redirection operators in linux.

1. > - redirects standard output to some file
2. >> - redirects the output to the file (Appends)
3. < - redirects standard input to some file

Examples -

```
cat abc.txt > xyz.txt
```

Above command will copy data from abc.txt to xyz.txt

```
cat abc.txt >> xyz.txt
```

Above command will copy data from abc.txt and append it into xyz.txt

```
wc -l < xyz.txt
```

Above command will read data from xyz.txt and print total number of lines in that file.

Tee command redirects output to the file as well as sends data in output stream

/dev/null is a special device. If you try to to redirect your data in that device, nothing will be stored.

23. Pipes

Pipe is a very important concept in Linux. With the help of Pipes, output from one command can be used as an input as the other command.

For example - Consider a scenario wherein you want to view all files whose name starts with letter s in sorted order. We can accomplish this task using 2 commands as shown below.

1. Find files starting with s.
2. Sort the list.

Command to do this is -

```
$find -name 's*' | sort
```

Explanation - find command generates the list of files matching given conditions. The output of the command is displayed on the standard output i.e console. But in above case, since we have used pipe (|), output of the command is sent as input to the sort command.

Another example - Let us say you want to number each line in the file. Then you can use below command to do it.

```
cat abc.txt | nl
```

xargs and pipes

xargs is very handy command to work on multiple files. It is usually used along with pipes.

24. Package Managers in Linux

Package managers are used to package and distribute the Linux applications.

In Linux, there are mainly 2 types of package managers.

1. Yum and RPM for Red Hat and CentOS
2. apt-get for Ubuntu and Debian based systems

Syntax for yum is given below.

yum install <package-name>
yum update <package-name>
yum remove <package-name>

Syntax for rpm is given below.

rpm -ivh <rpm-file>
rpm -uvh <rpm-file>
rpm -ev <package-name>

Syntax for apt-get is given below.

apt-get install <package-name>
apt-get update <package-name>
apt-get remove <package-name>

25. Shell scripting Introduction

Shell scripting is the language in linux which can be used to do some tasks by automation.

It is basically a combination of commands along with loops, conditional statements and functions.

We can perform most of the tasks by command line in linux but sometimes logic could get more complicated where programming is required and that's when linux shell scripting takes over. If you are familiar with any programming language like c, c++, python etc, then you will find it very simple to learn the shell scripting.

Benefits of shell scripting

1. gives you full control over the logic
2. provides programming constructs like conditional statements, loops, arrays, variables, functions
3. write once, use multiple times

26. Tools required for shell scripting

All you will need for linux scripting is the shell and it comes built in along with any linux distributions. So go ahead and install the linux on your system.

How to open the shell?

Depending upon your distribution, you can open the shell. The default shell is located in the **/bin/bash** directory. Or you can launch it from Desktop GUI as well. There are a lot of other type of shells. You can choose any of them.

How to check your shell details?

You can execute below commands to get more details about shell.

1. echo $SHELL
2. echo $0

27. First shell script

You should remember below things while writing the scripts.

1. Every script should being with "#!/bin/bash"
2. Comments can be added by prefixing the line with #

We are going to write a simple program in our first script. Write below lines of code in a file and name it as sample1.sh

```
#!/bin/bash

x=10

echo $x
```

Before you execute above command, ensure that you modify the permission of the file sample1.sh so that you can execute it.

```
chmod +x sample1.sh
```

To execute this program, just go to the shell prompt and type ./sample1.sh

```
This should generate below output.

10
```

28. Interacting with user

You can take input from the user using read command. Below program will prompt you to enter your name and once you enter your name, it will be printed back on to the screen.

```
echo "Please enter your name "
read your_name
echo "Your name is : $your_name"
```

We can read the data from standard input and initialize multiple variables as well

```
read name age city
echo "name = $name age = $age city = $city"
```

When we do not specify the name of variable, read command will assign the value to special variable "REPLY"

```
read
echo "You entered  $REPLY"
```

To prevent new lines, you can use "-en" option with echo command.

```
echo -en "Please enter your name "
read your_name
echo "Your name is : $your_name"
```

Using different field separator

```
IFS=@
```

echo "Enter the 2 values delimited by @ and then hit enter key"

```
read a b

echo "Value of a is $a"

echo "Value of b is $b"
```

29. Operators

There are lot of interesting operators in shell scripting that you don't find in other languages.

1. Arithmetic
2. Relational
3. Logical
4. File

Arithmetic operators

In arithmetic operators, we have +, - , /, *, %, = etc.

Relational operators

In relational operators, we have below operators.

1. -lt (less than), -gt(greater than), -le(less than or equal to), -ge(greater than or equal to), -eq (equal to), -ne (not equal to). We should use these operators in [ ]
2. We also have <, >, <=, >=, == and != operators. We should use these operators with double square brackets [[ ]]

[[ ]] is an extension of []. Double brackets are not POSIX complaint. So you should use it carefully as same script may not work on all other shells.

```
paul@paul-VirtualBox:~$ [[ 2 < 4 ]]
paul@paul-VirtualBox:~$ echo $?
0
paul@paul-VirtualBox:~$ [[ 2 -lt 4 ]]
paul@paul-VirtualBox:~$ echo $?
0
paul@paul-VirtualBox:~$ [[ 2 -ne 4 && 4=4 ]]
paul@paul-VirtualBox:~$ echo $?
0
paul@paul-VirtualBox:~$ [[ 2 -ne 4 && ( 4 = 4 || 3 = 4) ]]
paul@paul-VirtualBox:~$ echo $?
0
paul@paul-VirtualBox:~$ [[ paul =~ pa.* ]]
paul@paul-VirtualBox:~$ echo $?
0
paul@paul-VirtualBox:~$ [[ paul =~ pa.*l ]]
paul@paul-VirtualBox:~$ echo $?
0
paul@paul-VirtualBox:~$ [[ paul =~ pa.*lr ]]
paul@paul-VirtualBox:~$ echo $?
1
```

operators-in-linux-bash-scripting

Below examples show how to compare string in Linux.

Here "-n" means not empty. "-z" means empty string.

```
paul@paul-VirtualBox:~$ [[ -n $s1 ]]
paul@paul-VirtualBox:~$ echo $?
1
paul@paul-VirtualBox:~$ echo $s1

paul@paul-VirtualBox:~$ [[ $s1 = "" ]]
paul@paul-VirtualBox:~$ echo $s1

paul@paul-VirtualBox:~$ echo $?
0
paul@paul-VirtualBox:~$ s1=sa
paul@paul-VirtualBox:~$ [[ $s1 = "" ]]
paul@paul-VirtualBox:~$ echo $?
1
paul@paul-VirtualBox:~$ [[ -z $s1 ]]
paul@paul-VirtualBox:~$ echo $?
1
```

string-comparison-in-linux

Logical operators

We have below logical operators.

1. &&
2. ||

File Operators

In file operators, we have lot of operators that allow us to check if file is read only, executable or empty etc.

To check if file exists, you can use below command.

```
[[ -e f1.txt ]]
```

Above command has an exit status as 0 if file "f1.txt" exists.

We can use many options as mentioned below to check various attributes of a file.

1. -d : We can use this option to check for directory existence.
2. -G : This option is used to check if file is owned by specific group.
3. -r : This option is used to check there is read permission on file. Exit status is 0 if read permission is available.
4. -s : This option is used to check if size of file is not 0. Exit status is 0 if size of file not zero.
5. -w : This option is used to check there is write permission on file. Exit status is 0 if write permission is available.

6. -x : This option is used to check there is execute permission on file. Exit status is 0 if execute permission is available.

30. Special characters in BASH scripting

Before jumping into BASH scripting, it is very important to know special characters in BASH.

Here is the list of special characters in BASH.

1. # -> This character (hash) is used for marking the comments in shell script
2. ; -> This character (semi-colon) is used to separate 2 BASH commands.
3. ;; -> This is used in select case construct to mark the end of case block.
4. . -> This character (dot) is used to indicate current directory. If used in regular expressions, it matches exactly one character. The files with names starting with "." are treated as hidden files.
5. " " and ' ' -> Double quotes are used to preserve the spaces and identify special characters. Single quotes are used to preserve everything as it is. Variable value substitution does not work
6. / -> This character (forward slash) is used as path separator. For example - /etc/passwd. This character is also used as division operator in arithmetic operations.
7. \ -> This character (backward slash) is used to escape following character
8. ` -> backquote is used to execute the command and return the result
9. : -> This character(colon) is used as field separator in /etc/passwd file and in PATH variable
10. ! -> This character (exclamation mark) is used to invoke commands from bash history. This is also used as not equal to operator (!=)
11. * -> This character (star or asterisk) is used to match anything during filename expansion. This is also used in regular expressions to match zero or more occurrences of

preceding character. Additionally this character is also used as multiplication operator.

12. ** -> This set of characters are used as exponentiation operator.
13. ? -> This character is used as condition operator. In regular expressions, it matches o or 1 character.
14. $ -> This character is used as variable substitution. In regular expressions, it matches end of line.
15. $*, $@ -> These set of characters are used to access all positional parameters in one go. We can access each argument separately like $0 - script name, $1 - first parameter ...and so on.
16. $? -> This is used to access the exit status of last BASH command.
17. $$ -> This is used to get the current process id.
18. = -> This is used during assignment of value to the variable. This is also used to compare 2 strings or integers.
19. < -> This symbol is used as Input redirection. It is also used as "less than" comparison operator.
20. > -> This symbol is used as output redirection. It is also used as "greater than" comparison operator.
21. >> -> This symbol is used as output redirection. Data is appended to the file.
22. & -> This character is used to run job in the background. For example - "ls &"
23. - -> This character is used as minus sign in arithmetic operations. It is also used in cd command like "cd -" which takes you to previous working directory.
24. + -> This is used as addition operator in arithmetic operations.

Now let use look at some more complex special characters.

, -> This character is used for concatenation of strings.

$() -> Used for command substitution. Command inside parenthesis is executed and assigned to variable on left side. for example data=$(ls). This is also used for defining functions. This is also used for declaring array.

{} -> They are used for parameter expansions. They are also used in xargs and find command as well. For example - echo {a..e} This command will print values a, b,c,d,e

[] -> This is used to access array element. They are also used to define the character classes. They are also used in condition statements. Some of the operators are -eq, -lt, -gt, -a (logical and operator), -o (logical or operator).

(( )) -> Used to do arithmetic operations. Note that you do not need to use $ sign to access the variable values inside parenthesis.

[[ ]] -> This is used in conditional statements. You can use logical and operator (&&), logical or operator (||) and =~ (regular expression operator).

31. Variables in Linux BASH scripting

To create a variable, use below syntax. Please do not give spaces before or after = sign. In below example, we have created a variable with name "mypath" and assigned it a value "/etc".

```
mypath=/etc
cd "$mypath"
```

#below statement is same as above. It is recommended to use {} around the variable name to avoid getting errors.

```
cd "${mypath}"
```

#below command will print $mypath as it is. There will be no variable substitution.It preserves all characters in ' ' as it is.

```
cd '$mypath'
```

You can use below code to check if certain variable is a NULL or Not NULL. Here -z means return true if the variable is NULL.

```
if [ -z "$xyz" ]
then
echo "\$xyz is NULL."
fi
```

We can also assign values to the variables using below syntax.

```
lsoutput=`ls -l`
echo $lsoutput

lsoutput=$(ls)

a=100
let "a = a+ 1"

echo $a
```

To display current bash version, you can use below enviornment

```
echo $BASH_VERSION
```

Here is the list of some of the important enviornment variables.

1. $CDPATH - list of search paths available to the cd command.
2. $DIRSTACK - top most value in stack used with pushd and popd.
3. $OLDPWD - old working directory
4. $BASHPID - Current Bash PID
5. $OSTYPE - Operating system type
6. $PATH - PATH variable contains the list of paths seperated by :
7. $SHLVL - Shell level

Note that environment variables are accessible to any script in the system.

declare command in Linux

You can use declare command to declare the variables with special attributes.

We can declare read only variable using below syntax.

```
declare -r pi=3.14
```

We can declare integer variable using below syntax.

```
declare -i age=22
```

We can declare array using below syntax.

```
declare -a myarray
```

We can define the function using below syntax.

```
declare -f functionName
```

declare is also used for printing all variables.

set command in Linux

set command is used to do below things.

1. display all variables.
2. It is also used to set the positional parameters.
3. It is also used to modify the internal shell variables.

unset command in Linux

unset command is used to delete the variable.

export command in Linux

export command is used to make the variable available to all child shell and processes.

typeset command in Linux

typeset command is used to change the variable attributes.

Read only variables

We can create read only variables in 2 ways.

1. declare -r variable1
2. readonly variable1

32. Arrays

In this topic, you will learn how to work with arrays in Linux.

Creating new array variable

When you create variable using [], you are actually creating array.

```
cities[0]='Brisbane'
cities[1]='Perth'

echo "Element at position 1 in an array"
 ${cities[1]}
```

Alternatively, you an create array using below syntax.

```
declare -a cities=(Brisbane Perth)
```

Another way to create an array is by loading data from file using below syntax. In below example, cities array will be created by loading data from the file - "cities.txt" Note that each element is same as each line in a file.

```
cities=( `cat "cities.txt" `)
```

Adding elements in array

Adding new element in array is also very simple. For example - If you want to add element at position number 2, you can use below syntax.

```
cities[2]='Perth'
```

Accessing elements in array

```
echo "Element at position 1 in an array"
 ${cities[1]}

echo "All elements in an array"
 ${cities[@]}
```

Finding the size of array

You can use below syntax to find total number of elements in an array.

```
echo "All elements in an array"
 ${#cities[@]}
```

Removing elements in array

You can use below syntax to delete an element in array. Below statement will delete an element at position 2.

```
unset cities[2]
```

Copying elements in an array

You can use below syntax to copy array. Here elements of array cities are copied into array - "towns"

```
towns=("${cities[@]}")
```

Joining arrays

```
newarray=("${cities[@]}" "${towns[@]}")
echo ${newarray[@]}
```

Replacing the data of an element in array

You can use below syntax to replace the contents of an element in an array.

```
echo ${cities[@]/Per/Ade}
```

Iterating through the array elements

```
for (( i=0;i<${#cities[@]};i++)); do
echo ${cities[${i}]}
done
```

33. Arithmetic operations

33.1 Integer operations

You can use below ways to do integer operations in Linux.

b=2

1. a=`expr $b + 1`
2. a=$((b+2))
3. let a=b-1

33.2 floating point operations

In this topic, let us learn how to perform operations on floating point numbers in Linux.

We know that we can use below ways to perform operations on Integer numbers.

1. a=`expr $b + 1`
2. a=$((b+2))
3. let a=b-1

If you try to use floating point numbers in above commands, you will get error saying "non-integer argument"

In Linux, we can use "bc" command to perform operations on floating point numbers as shown in below examples.

```
a=$(echo 2.3 + 3.4 |   bc)
```

34. String manipulation in shell scripting

This topic covers various ways in which we can manipulate strings in BASH scripting.

Finding the length of the variable's value

All of below commands will print the length of the value of variable "city"

```
city=Brisbane
echo ${#city}
echo `expr length $city`
echo `expr "$city" : '.*'`
```

Finding the sub string position

Below commands print the length of matching substring

```
echo `expr match "$city" 'Bris'`
echo `expr "$city" : 'Bris*'`
```

Finding the index of first character

```
echo `expr index "$city" b233`
echo `expr index "$city" 5n`
```

Extract the portion of the string

1. echo ${city:0}
2. echo ${city:1}
3. echo ${city:2:4}
4. echo ${city:(-4)}
5. echo ${city: -4}

You can also use expr to return the sub string.

```
echo `expr substr $city 1 3`
echo `expr substr $city 2 4`
```

Extracting arguments of the script

```
echo ${*:2}
echo ${@:2}
echo ${*:1:2}
```

Getting matched pattern

```
echo `expr match "$city" '\(.*sb\)'`
echo `expr "$city" : '\(.*sb\)'`
```

Delete the shortest and longest match from the beginning of the string

```
echo ${stringZ#a*C}
echo ${stringZ##a*C}
```

Delete the shortest and longest match from the end of the string

```
${city%b}
${city%%s}
```

Replace the sub string

```
${string/substring/replacement}
${string//substring/replacement}

echo ${city/bane/boon}
```

35. Substitutions

35.1 Parameter substitution

In this topic, you will learn how to substitute the parameters.

```
firstName=paul
lastName=watson

fullName=${firstName} ${HOSTNAME}
echo "$fullName"
```

Default parameters

In case, the variable is not initialized (null), you may want to use default value.
You can use below syntax to specify the default value for the parameter.

${parameter-defaultValue} - This means that if the parameter is not declared, use defaultValue

${parameter:-defaultValue} - This means that if the parameter is declared and it's value is null, use defaultValue
Below command will print 2 as we have not declared num

```
echo ${num-2}

num=
```

Below command will print 2 as we have declared num but the value is null

```
echo ${num:-2}

num=111
```

Below command will print 111 as we have declared num and it's value is not null.

```
echo ${num:-2}
```

Print error message if variable is not declared or is null

If the variable is not declared, Error_Message is printed.

```
${variable?Error_Message}
```

In below syntax, if the variable is declared and it is null, Error_Message is printed.

```
${parameter:?Error_Message}
```

Printing the length of variable value

Below statement will print length of variable. If it is array, it returns the length of the first element in the array.

```
${#variable}
```

Deleting the shortest and longest matching pattern from the beginning of the variable

```
# means it will delete the shortest
matching pattern.

${variable#pattern}

## means it will delete the longest
matching pattern.

${variable##pattern}
```

Deleting the shortest and longest matching pattern from the end of the variable

```
% means it will delete the shortest
matching pattern.

${variable%pattern}

%% means it will delete the longest
matching pattern.

${variable%%pattern}
```

Replacing the pattern

```
/ means replace the first occurrence of the
pattern.

${variable/Pattern/Replacement}

// means replace all the occurrences of the
pattern.

${variable//Pattern/Replacement}
```

Below command can be used to replace the pattern only if prefix matches the pattern.

```
${variable/#Pattern/Replacement}
```

Below command can be used to replace the pattern only if prefix matches the pattern.

```
${variable/%Pattern/Replacement}
```

35.2 Command Substitution

Command substitution in Linux Shell Scripting can be done in 2 ways.

1. x=`ls`
2. x=$(ls)

In command substitution, output of the command is assigned to the variable.

36. Statements

36.1 Conditional statements

You can use if else statements using below syntax

```
if [ condition ]
then
statements...
elif [ condition ]
statements...
else
statements...
fi
```

Condition can be any of the value.

1. -eq -> Eqality operator
2. -ne ->Non-Equality Operator
3. -gt -> greater than operator
4. -ge -> greater than or equal operator
5. -lt -> less than
6. -le -> less than or equal to

Examples on if statement

```
if [ "$mypath" == "/etc" ]
then
        echo "mypath variable is equal to
/etc"
else
        echo "mypath variable is not equal
to /etc"
fi
```

If you want to put "then" keyword in the same line, you will have to use semicolon after if condition.

```
a=11
b=22
if [ "$a" -eq 11 ] && [ "$b" -eq 22 ]
then
          echo "Both conditions are true"
else
          echo "One or both of the
conditions are true"
fi


if [ "$a" -eq 11 ] || [ "$b" -eq 23 ]
then
          echo "One or Both of the
conditions are true"
else
          echo "Both conditions are false"
fi
```

When grep command finds at least one pattern in a file, it returns 0 (condition is true)

```
if grep -q pattern myfile
then echo "pattern found in myfile"
fi
```

cmp command returns 0 when 2 files are same (condition is true).

```
if cmp f1 f2 &> /dev/null
then
        echo "File f1 and f2 are same."
else
        echo "File f1 and f2 are not
same."
fi
```

Conditional operator in Linux

? operator works in the same as in Java language.

Syntax of ? operator is given below.

```
var = <condition> ?
<trueValue>:<falseValue>
```

If the condition is true, trueValue is assigned to variable "var".
If the condition is false, falseValue is assigned to variable "var".

For example -

below statement is same as the if else block that follows.

```
(( a = b > 3 ? 1:2 ))

if [ b -gt 3 ]
then
          a=1
else
        a=2
fi
```

Case statements

Case statements are similar to switch ...case statements in C language. Here is the syntax. Note that we need to use ;; to mark the end of case block.

```
case "$switch" in

1) echo "Case 1" ;;

2) echo "Case 2" ;;

esac
```

36.2 Looping statements

We can use below looping statements in Linux shell scripting.

1. while
2. for

while loop

```
while <condition>
do
statements....
done
```

Here is an example on while loop. Below loop will print values from 1 to 10.

```
count=1

while [ "$count" -le 10 ]
do
echo $count

# let "count += 1"
((count = count + 1))
done
```

for loop

Here are some of the examples on for loop.

```
for i in 1 2 3 4 5
do
echo "value of i is $i"
done

for i in {1..3}
do
echo "value of i is $i"
done

for (( i=1; i<=3; i++ ))
do
echo "Value of i -> $i"
done
```

Below code will kill all process that match pattern - "myPattern"

```
for KILLPID in `ps ax | grep 'myPattern' |
awk ' { print $1;}'`; do
kill -9 $KILLPID;
done

for KILLPID in `pgrep anyprocessname`; do
kill -9 $KILLPID;
done
```

37. Passing data in and out of shell script

37.1 Passing parameters

We can pass the parameters (arguments) to shell script delimited by white spaces. You can access the current script name and arguments using $0, $1,$2....and so on.

```
$0 = Script name (also called as base name of file)

$1 = First argument to the script

$2 = Second argument to the script and so on..
```

In the script, we can access count of arguments using $#

```
if [ $# < 2 ]
then
          echo "Count of parameters is less than 2"
exit -1
fi
```

We can use below special variables to access the parameters.

1. $@ - All of the arguments.
2. $* - All of the arguments. This does not preserve the white space and quotes.

Another variables that start with $ are given below.

1. $$ - This gives you the process id of current shell.
2. $! - This gives you the process id of last background process.

37.2 exit status of the script

Every shell script returns a value.

When it returns 0 value, it means that script was run successfully.
But if it returns non-zero value, it means that script did not run as expected.Non-zero value actually indicates the error code.

You can use "exit" command to return a value from the script.

Both of the below commands are equal.

```
exit
exit $?
```

You can even omit "exit" statement at the end of script as it is added implicitly by BASH.

If you use pipes, then $? will give you the result of only last command in the pipe. To get the exit status of every command, you can use PIPESTATUS variable.

```
$ false | true ; echo ${PIPESTATUS[0]}

$ false | true | false; echo
${PIPESTATUS[*]}
```

When script or command is successful, it returns 0. But since the command is successful, it is considered to be true when checking the condition.

When script or command fails, it returns non zero value (1). But since the command has failed, it is considered to be false when checking the condition.

38. Functions

Main use of functions is that we can reuse the same code and we can call the same function many times.

We can write functions in shell scripts, using below syntax. To call the function, you can just use the name of the function as a command. Note that definition of the function should appear first in a bash file and then we can call the function. If you try to call the function before defining it, you will get an error saying "command not found"

```
f1 ()
{
echo "This is a simple function in Linux
shell scripting"
}

f1
```

39. Sourcing files

"source" command is used to source any valid shell script file. Here is the syntax of source command.

```
source <script-file-name>
```

Main purpose of source command is that we can use functions or commands defined in another file in any other script or from in shell prompt.

Note that if you want to execute any script file, you should have a execute permission on that file. But When you use "source" command, you do not need to have a execute permission on that file.

Suppose you have simple script file - "s1.sh" with below contents

```
ls
```

Now to execute "s1.sh", you can use below command.

```
$ source s1.sh
```